The old man sits quietly on the beach as he watches hundreds of starfish wash up on shore, the tide leaving them behind to die. He looks across the beach to see a young man rushing toward the hundreds of starfish. As fast as the young man can, he picks up one starfish at a time and begins throwing them back into the ocean. The old man in such dismay calls out to the young man.

"Hey, can't you see that's an endless battle. You can't make a difference. There are way too many."

The young man, never stopping to address the older man, reaches down and picks up another starfish, throws it back into the ocean and yells back to the old man, "Made a difference for that one."

author unknown

The old man sits quietly on the beach as he watches hundreds of starfish wash up on shore, the tide leaving them behind to die. He looks across the beach to see a young man rushing toward the hundreds of starfish. As fast as the young man can, he picks up one starfish at a time and begins throwing them back into the ocean. The old man in such dismay calls out to the young man.

"Hey, can't you see that's an endless battle. You can't make a difference. There are way too many."

The young man, never stopping to address the older man, reaches down and picks up another starfish, throws it back into the ocean and yells back to the old man, "Made a difference for that one."

author unknown

An Exercise in Going Home to Your Heart

ROUNDTRIP TICKET

Belanie Dishong

In order to preserve my friends' and students' privacy, certain names have been changed.

This book is available at special quantity discounts for bulk purchases for sales promotions, premiums, fund-raising, and educational needs. Special books or book excerpts also can be created to fit specific needs. For details, write Limitless Living Publishing at 7710-T Cherry Park Drive Box 310, Houston, TX 77095.

The Library of Congress has cataloged the
hardback edition as follows:
Dishong, Belanie.

Roundtrip Ticket:
An Exercise in Going Home to Your Heart /
Belanie Dishong.

ISBN 10: 0-9790756-0-2
ISBN 13: 978-0-9790756-0-5
1. Authorship. I Title.

First edition, October 2006
10 9 8 7 6 5 4 3 2 1

This book is printed on acid-free paper.

Book design by Ying Pee Eng, Jian Design Ltd.
Book cover photography by Brooke Duthie Photography.
Edited by Carrie Koch.
Copyedited by Melissa Bachara.

The Reason I've Written This Book

As the starfish story has been passed on and shared through the years, the impression it made on me is indelible and it best represents my purpose: to make a difference, one heart at a time. Always keeping this story in mind, I move forward each day. It represents to me the true meaning of serving.

Dedication

This book is dedicated to my first family: Dad; Mom; my brothers, Bob (Robert), Butch (Gordon), and Buddy (Hollis); and my sister Brenda. No matter where I have been, or what I have done throughout my life they have always been my cheerleaders. I am so grateful for our time together. Though Dad, Mom, and Buddy have moved on in their journey of life I am ever so present to their continued cheers. Each of you contributed to me and I want you to know I am honored to be your daughter and sister.

Gratitude

God, I offer my greatest gratitude for the

Abundant gift of choice,
Grace to honor choice as a gift,
Clarity of life through choice,
Equality available to all in life through choice,
And the Wisdom to share the gift of choice.

Everything there is to be, to do, and to have in life is A Matter of Choice, for which I give my humble thanks.

Acknowledgments

I am certain that taking my dream to write this book to the reality of you reading it is in great part due to the enormous love, encouragement, and talents of so many wonderful people in my life. I feel such joy that I can take this time to honor them for what they have done and for who they are in my life.

To my precious husband, Doug, thank you for everything that you bring to my life, particularly your everlasting support, understanding, and unconditional love. I love you.

To the greatest children a mother could ever dream of having, Mike, Bridget, Nicole, and Eric: Thank you for all the years of loving me no matter what, cheering me on, and believing in me. You guys are the world to me.

Mike, thank you for your inspiration and creativity in naming *Roundtrip Ticket: An Exercise in Going Home to the Heart*. It is perfect.

The lights of my life are the purest of them all: my grandchildren. The joy I know through them is priceless. Allie, Maddie, and Noah, you are so precious to me and I am thankful to God that I get to be your Gram.

Bill Ferguson, my mentor and one of my dearest friends, thank you for all that you have done to light my path. I am honored that you would consider me your peer.

Joyce Brown, thank you for your request and encouragement to go forward with this work so many years ago. It is through that, I have discovered my purpose and my passion. I will never forget your support and encouragement that opened the door to today.

Paige Bearce-Beery and Lydia Barrett, through

all the years I know that no matter what you are there for me. Your encouragement is invaluable. Thank you for your unwavering faith and belief in me.

Lon Fiala, my business partner and friend, thank you for believing in me and Live at Choice. Your coaching inspired me to push for my dream for Live at Choice no matter what, and never stop.

I am forever indebted to an unbelievable team of leaders, for their commitment to me, to this work, and to the quality of life for others. Words can not truly express the gratitude that I feel for the support that they have given and continue to give. Thank you all: Paige Bearce-Beery, Lydia Barrett, Susan Bender, Carrie Koch, Kathy Rich, Monica Wellington, Doug Dishong, Lon Fiala, and Ken VanTuyl.

Carrie, a special thanks to you: All of your hours of hard work are so appreciated. Your overwhelming commitment to live your life as an example of this work is such an inspiration to me and others. You walk the walk, lady, thanks. And to Sophie...thank you for putting up with your mom's long hours, and for your willingness to chip in where needed. You're a real trooper, and a great example of this work for young people.

Thank you to thirteen years worth of incredible people, sharing their lives, discovering who they truly are, and living their lives from their hearts. You are an inspiration.

Thank you, Charles, Joe, Bill, and Charlie for your huge contribution in my life. You are all very special to me.

Jay Silverman, thank you for your introductions and encouragements. You are a friend indeed.

Ray Cheng and the team at Jian Global Services, thank you for all that you have done and continue to do to bring this work to the world. You are all greatly appreciated. You have made a difference to this one.

Table of Contents

Preface

This book is dedicated to all who dream a dream and never stop dreaming, to those who have yet to dream, for those who dreamed and have given up on their dreams, and to those who are afraid to dream. I dedicate this book to you, for it is your dreams that I live to see realized.

Reasons for you to read this book:

Imagine: What would the world be like if everyone were living their dreams and living from their hearts?

Imagine: What if you were living from your dreams? Really stop and imagine.

Questions to be answered:

- Two people made a million dollars in the stock market, the market crashes. One commits suicide. The other goes on the make another million. Why?
- Why are so many of our teens suffering from image disaster?
- Why are divorce rates rising?
- Why are so many relationships experienced as painful?
- Why are people working more, working harder, and enjoying it less?

The list is endless.

Imagine discovering the answers.

Roundtrip Ticket will challenge you to look at the way you ordinarily view life. It is going to introduce to you to the fact that you can declare the way you experience life and create your circumstances ahead of you, rather than be at the mercy of what life seems to throw at you.

You'll be encouraged to re-engage yourself with the dreams that fuel your heart find those dreams and empower them, living your life from a singing heart. You'll begin to discover that you have defined certain things about yourself that have you see life in a particular way. It is these same self-defined outlooks that have you fall short of living your dreams.

Through real-life stories you will see how these decisions have shaped people's lives, made their choices, and created everything going on in their experiences. You will see how they discovered these decisions, embraced them, and stopped resisting them. Through this process they discovered that a large part of their everyday lives had been about trying to disprove their self-defined outlooks. Once they embraced these aspects of themselves, they were free to see all of their options and therefore created their circumstances so that they began to truly realize their dreams.

It is interesting to see that none of us is exempt from having made decisions about ourselves. These decisions are made very early in life. We have attributed our explanation for how our lives have turned out to our social, economic, parental, and cultural fortunes or misfortunes. This book has you begin to look at the possibility that maybe it is not the circumstances in our lives that has made the difference, but rather it is what we made the circumstances mean about ourselves that has made the greatest impact in the way our lives have turned out.

It's a journey, come along...

Leap Forward – Create It Now

Why are you here? What do you want to get out of participating in this book? These are pretty interesting questions coming from the beginning of a book. After all, how could you possibly know what you were going to get from a book that you haven't even read? Well hang on - this is a new adventure, possibly even a new way to be, a new venture, a joint-venture with life. There is truly a partnership relationship between you and every element in your life. Are you going to take it on?

What if you had the opportunity to declare something to be gained in everything that you approach, be it a book, a movie, a course, a workshop, a walk, a new acquaintance, a new relationship, a conversation with an old friend? How about that sales call you are about to make, the big meeting coming up, the speech you are about to give?

Every aspect of your day could be about deciding how it is going to be with no evidence of it being possible. What a powerful way to begin to live your life. Speaking and creating what you want as an outcome before you get there, rather than giving a report and assessment once the event has been experienced. Let's just call this experiencing with an intended and pre-declared value a Leap Forward.

So now, what is your reason for being here? What is it that you intend to get out of being a participant in this book? "Participant?" You may be asking yourself. "How on earth am I a participant? I am just reading this book."

What if you were to approach this book as a participant in the material and the outcome rather than an observer? What might be of value that you may not see or hear if you approach this book simply as a reader, as an observer of the information?

If you were to have an intended outcome and you were to actively participate in the journey of this book, you would then be responsible for the outcome, rather than looking for the book to provide the answer. Maybe you could produce the same results in all aspects of your life. What if there were a new way for you to be accountable for your outcomes in life?

Welcome to the journey, the path with no end, the place of true choice, living from your heart. No more trying to get better. No more getting over things or trying to overcome, but rather a place of finding and living the truth - living from your heart. Consider that this might mean you will get the chance to come full circle and return to who you truly are - no changing required here! Engaging in this journey gives you a chance to live a life free of upset, no longer strapped by fear, seeing more clearly what you want out of life, and stepping up to the plate to make it happen.

Let's go back to the original questions. Why are you here, and what do you want to get out of participating in this book?

If you haven't already answered these questions, stop and do so now. Take out a piece of paper and start with the first question; why are you here? Why did you choose to pick up this book? Where are you in your life that you want to read this book? What is the reason that you were drawn to this book? What is that? What could be different for you that might make your life more fulfilled? Look deeper into these questions than you may have ever looked before.

Why are you here? Let's see, you have probably spent some money to purchase this book, and now you are going to invest some of your valuable time in reading it. Consider these investments. If you could have anything, what would you choose?

You can have anything...so let's get to creating now. Get risky! Choose something in which there is no apparent evidence that you could possibly have what you choose as an outcome for "just reading a book." What is it that you would have become possible - more loving relationships, time for yourself, living a stress-free life, the direction for financial freedom? You name it.

Here are a few hints to stretch your imagination. When you decide what your outcome will be, remove all the want, need, and will be-type words and replace them with I am and I have-type words. This is a huge Leap Forward for most people. You have probably heard, read, or imagined such a possibility, but never given it any true thought or applied it to your life. Now suddenly, you have stumbled upon an opportunity to test it for yourself.

One of the lessons of this book is for each of us to learn and experience that we can, in fact, say in advance what we are going to be, to do, and to have, and see it happen. What we don't realize is that we are making those statements already each and every moment, but we just aren't aware of the link between our words and their impact on our outcomes.

There's a saying, "If you want to know where you will be in five years, listen to your thoughts and speaking."

Truer words were never spoken. The discovery is in finding the author of our thoughts and our speaking.

We know that we place our focus on what we think and what we speak. Therefore, the result is that we will in fact realize that upon which we focus. This book is not about giving you this information yet again, but rather about finding the author of the thoughts and therefore, the speaking that results in the focus. Why do we think and speak as we do? Let's look for and find the author.

Now you have recognized the intended value of participating in this book.

What all did you notice about doing this exercise?

What exactly were the questions that went through your mind as you began trying to find answers?

Did you notice a resistance to saying what you wanted? After all, what if it doesn't happen? Then what?

What doubts popped up for you during the exercise?

Jot down the thoughts you were having as you digested the questions and looked for the answers. It will be good reference for you later in the book.

You are, after all, now a participant, and not just a reader and observer of this book. You now have a vested interest in the outcome. There is accountability on your part to have a valued result from participating in this book.

As you journey through the book you will begin to see that this accountability is actually you becoming 100 percent responsible for every outcome in your life. Not at all like fault, but actually becoming the cause and living your life very powerfully "causing by choice."

You will see where and how choice is originated and how you truly impact your own circumstances. When you authentically join in on life and become partner and participant in the journey, knowing that you do create the way life presents itself, then you are truly in a joint-venture with life. What an adventure!

Let's go.

Direction by Design - The Dream

A goal without a dream is a task-driven life, falling just short of the top of the mountain. Most often when we reach our goals, we feel a sense of accomplishment and then try to find the next goal to conquer.

Why is this dream stuff so important? When you were a child the sky was the only limit. You knew that in life everything was possible. Then there came a time when you began to define your limitations. You developed Limiting Thinking, followed only by Limited Living.

As I work with new participants in workshops, we often discover that they keep their dreams carefully tucked away and hold them in a place that is unattainable. Most of the time, they don't even start out acknowledging that they have dreams. If they do, they have usually given up on these dreams becoming reality. Whose conversation are you living when it comes to defining, going for, and obtaining your dreams?

Many of us grew up believing we should be practical in the direction we took our lives. Practicality and dreams really never came in the same package. Education, followed by a good job, starting a family, and making something of ourselves usually were not synonymous with "living our dreams," unless, of course, those were our actual dreams. We then would say that we had realized our dreams. For most of us, living out dreams was something that very few people did. The really big question is: Why do some people live their dreams, while others do not?

We will see this question many times throughout the book. Why some? Why not others? At this point we might attribute it to parental influence, to the times, or we may say it was just what we were supposed to do.

There was one workshop participant who said, "I don't want to have my dreams, because if I did then I wouldn't have anything to live for. That's what keeps me going, always having it out there."

After some work, he realized that he wasn't telling himself the truth. Actually, he so very much wanted to have his dream, but he had an enormous amount of evidence that it was not possible. If he were to actually say he was going to have it, and he didn't get it, then he would have been a failure. That was too big of a price to pay. Once he was able to see what the truth really was for him, then he could begin to see when and why he had decided that it could never come true.

How do you hold dreams? Can you make a list of your dreams? Can you feel the energy around the possibility of those dreams? Can you see them in your mind's eye? Do you know what it would be like living your dreams right now?

Think about it this way, if you could have just one of your dreams come true and you could live everyday through your dream, would your heart sing? Would you jump up out of bed excited about life? Can you imagine if you were living that dream how much of your life would be coming from pure joy? If the answer is yes, then that is the direction, the dream that I want you to go for with all your might, regardless of all the circumstances, conditions, and situations proving that it's not possible. If you have several, which is certainly possible, then choose the one that would most make your heart sing if it were real right now. Put it down on paper; make it real for yourself. Keep the dream out in front at all times. Empower the dream. "Feed your faith and your doubts will starve to death." You can have the dream.

I believe and often share with my participants that you can create anything you can dream. If you can dream it, you can have it. The only thing between you and realizing your dreams is you saying so. If this is true, then why don't you say so?

Let's open the door to identifying the author

of what we say is so. When we say our dreams are not obtainable, we then assign the circumstances to substantiate that being the truth. What we get is more evidence and more circumstances of proof that we can not have the dream.

When we say our dreams are obtainable, we then assign the circumstances to substantiate that being the truth and what we get is more evidence and more circumstances that we can have it. We continue doing so until the dream has become the reality.

This is the basic, fundamental law of attraction. You will attract into your life what you say is so.

Knowing and Its Effect on Choice - A Profound Discovery

How often do you say, "Well I choose this or I chose that? It was my choice!"

Let's take a real good look at this thing called choice. Pick a time that you last looked at something and had to decide if you were going to do it or not. What happened while you were making the decision?

- Did you weigh all the options?
- Did you weigh the possible consequences?
- Did you look at what could happen if you declined?
- Did you look at what would happen if you accepted or chose to do it?

It's perfectly fine to look at all the options as you make your choice, but did you ever hear the words:

- I am afraid of _________ if I do this.
- I am afraid of ________ if I don't do this.
- What will people think of me if I do this?
- What will people think of me if I don't do this?
- I really can't do that.
- What if I screw it up?
- It's easier to just not do it.

What were the thoughts and questions you were hearing as you were trying to choose? Let's look at the origin of those questions. Why on earth do you even have those questions? After all, how many times have you been told not to base your life on what others might think of you? Maybe you have even been told to jump out there and choose. Don't let your fears stop you.

Then of course, there are thousands of other

questions or considerations that might have come to mind prior to making your decision. The point is, where do these questions come from?

We have been taught over and over that the questions are having good judgment, that we shouldn't make hasty or snap decisions. You remember all these lessons. But let's see if maybe that's not the source of these questions after all. As we continue in this journey of discovery together we will begin to look at other possible origins of these types of questions.

Consider that there are two realms of choice. One is conscious; the other is unconscious. A large part of our circumstances are a direct result of our unconscious choices. Oh certainly, it is you saying, "I choose this" or "I choose that," but most of these "choices" are not chosen from conscious options, but rather from no options. While you have lots of "reasons" for your choices, they are not coming from pure choice. We think these reasons are valid and that full consideration was given, which resulted in the choice made. "Due to the circumstances, I choose this."

Let's take a look for a moment at the "knowledge" we use to make our choices. Let's pretend that all there is to know fits in a really large pie pan. Now take and slice out a piece of pie about one-eighth the size of the pan. Let's assume for a moment that the space of that removed piece now holds all that you know that you know. To get a feel for this, answer this question: What do you know that you know? Let's say you know how to brush your teeth; you know how to do your job; you know where you live. You get the idea.

Now let's slice out a piece the size of one-quarter of the pan. So what's this? It is the amount knowledge that you know that you don't know. What are some of the things that you know that you don't know? I really do have a point here, so hang on. Unless you are a brain surgeon by profession, then it's pretty safe to say that you know that you don't know how to perform brain surgery. Correct? Take a moment and spend some time thinking about some of the things you know that you don't know.

My first suggestion here is that for each of us, from the beginning of life to now, we have spent most, if not all, of our life looking at what we know that we don't know and deciding what we want to know. Then we educated ourselves, gained experience, and practiced to increase our knowledge in the area of what we know that we know. Would you agree? As a result, our life gains a larger section of the pie in the area of what we know that we know. All the while, the slice of what we know that we don't know decreases.

That's pretty much what it's all about. When our decisions and choices are made from what we know that we know, then we are making conscious choices.

Hold on here a moment, what's in the rest of that pie pan? We have only looked at three-eighths of the pie, (one-eighth holding all the stuff that we know that we know, one-quarter holding all the stuff that we know that we don't know). There's a big piece of the pie missing. What resides in that other five-eights?

Its resident is the knowledge that causes your unconscious choice. It is the very place where many of our decisions are made and where our upsets are born. Normally, in our everyday living, we do not have access to this knowing - primarily because we don't even know that it exists. Let's call this what we don't know that we don't know. Let's go over that again. The largest portion of the pie is inhabited by information that, for a lack of better description, we don't even know that we don't know. When the information stored in this area is used in making our decisions we are living a life by default.

How does this happen and how does it exist? One of the most important things for me to pass on to you is that the circumstances, conditions, and situations in life are never, ever the problem. It is only what you make them mean about you that makes the defining mark. Here's an example:

There were two sisters who participated in one of my workshops. One of the sisters, Mary, was an accomplished singer as were with both of their parents. The other sister, Linda, said her voice was so bad that she wouldn't even sing in the shower. Mary agreed. Linda so much wanted to sing and felt all of her life that she had been cheated. As far back as she could remember, she dreamed of being able to sing with the rest of the family, but clearly she knew that she could never have that dream. In later years, it was so painful for Linda that she would avoid any event, big or small, even Christmas events, often times staying home. The entire family loved the opera, except Linda, of course. So off they would go and she chose to say home, because she "really wasn't interested."

One of the things Linda wanted to get out of participating in the workshop, her Leap Forward at the beginning of the event, was to be free of the resentment she had that her entire family could sing, but she did not have that gift.

As the workshop went on, she began to discover for herself that there was a time she could sing. She remembered loving to hear her voice as a very young girl. We began inquiring into the possibility that there could be something that she didn't know that she didn't know that might hold the answer. As we talked she recalled an event that the two girls entered when Linda was five and Mary was seven. There were a lot of children from the area doing various types of dances and singing for a local talent show. It was being recorded for the local TV station and was to be aired on the Jerry Lewis Telethon. The girls were so excited about seeing themselves on TV. Finally the night came for the show to air. She could see herself, her sister, their family and friends all gathered around the TV just waiting. They did not leave the room throughout the entire telethon. It was such fun seeing her sister and the other kids, but as the event came to an end the next morning, she never appeared on the show. She had been edited out of the show. She was more than devastated. It meant that she was "not good enough." She was not as good as her sister. The pain was so great that she could not bear how it felt.

From that moment on, she was certain that she could not sing. She was "not good enough," and never wanted to feel that pain again. No matter how much her parents tried to console her, she had already decided that she was "not good enough." Her singing voice was frozen in time from that moment.

"Not good enough" had become a part of what she didn't know that she didn't know. It framed all her decisions and choices around singing, music, and competition. In the area of music, she lived a life of "default" unconscious choice. She had no access to conscious choice, her design. The pain felt on that day of "not good enough" was so strong she was no longer free to choose. Not being talented and left out of the family's gift of singing became her limiting thinking and her limited living.

Let's visit the conditions of these circumstances. What really happened?

Fact 1: The event was not a competition and children were not eliminated based on their talent.

Fact 2: The TV network made edits based on time allotments for the show. Each time the local area was given a slot for raising money, they would air one or two of their local talents. At the time they shot the segments, the local stations were unaware of just how often the network would be showing local slots, so they filmed more than they thought they would possibly need for the telethon.

Fact 3: What Linda did not realize and never noticed was that many of the other children that were filmed that day had been cut as well.

Notice, that none of the FACTS made any difference in the conclusion she had drawn. Once she made the CIRCUMSTANCES MEAN SOMETHING about her, then her LIFE BECAME

ABOUT AVOIDING THE ORIGINAL PAIN surrounding that moment. From that time forward she told herself she did not like to sing and that she was not gifted with that talent.

A little further in the book we will discuss how it is that we set up the path to make sure we never feel that original pain again. But for now, let us just do a little review.

What do we now know that we know? Interesting, isn't it? We have actually moved something from what we didn't know that we didn't know into what we know that we know. This is called an insight. To clarify, the insight for us is that we have seen how our unconscious choices are made. The insight for Linda was that in that moment at the end of the telethon, she decided she was "not good enough." It begins with a decision that we make about a circumstance, situation, or event. Further, we have seen that the circumstances around the event really didn't, in truth, mean what Linda made them mean. No one said she was "not good enough." When she made that her reality, she stored it away and made every effort in her life from that point forward to ensure she never experienced that pain again.

Through this example, our insight is to see how we become locked into unconscious choice. When you have these insights, you have the opportunity for making conscious choice.

For you, as the participant in the book, your first new conscious choice, through this first insight, is that you get to choose to see what it is about you that you don't know that you don't know. For Linda, as long as the "not good enough" was buried in "what you don't know that you don't know," she had no possibility of singing or even enjoying anything having to do with singing and music. However, through her discovery, she could now explore the possibility of her singing voice.

To recap, so far, you have had the opportunity to see several new insights:

- Insight 1: We have discovered that in the realm of knowing we have three sections:
  - What we know that we know.
  - What we know that we don't know.
  - What we don't know that we don't know.

- Insight 2: We have discovered that there are two types of choices which frame the way we live our lives:
  - Conscious choice.
  - Unconscious choice.

- Insight 3: We have discovered that:
  - Conscious choices are choices made through what we know that we know.
  - Unconscious choices are choices made through what we don't know that we don't know.

- Insight 4: Going a step further, we have discovered that the circumstances, conditions, and events in our lives really aren't the problem, but it is WHAT WE MAKE THEM MEAN ABOUT OURSELVES THAT FRAMES OUR VIEW OF LIFE. I call this filtering.

If this is true, what is this process, and where do we go from here?

Life Inside the Illusion - View Through Filters

The illusion is thinking that we see life the "way that it really is." We, as the human race, are so certain about this that we go to war to prove how right we are about the "way that it is." Perhaps the only place that life is the way you see it, is in your own reality. Your reality is only a demonstration of your individual perception. No other person sees it exactly the way you do.

Taking it a step further, again consider that the way you see life is based absolutely on your view through your filters. I call these your core filters. It's like wearing a pair of glasses that show you preconceived ideas of what is so. We all have them, as we saw earlier.

Linda looked at the circumstances around the TV show and decided that she was "not good enough." The "not good enough" became one of her core filters. Was it the truth? No, it was just her individual perception of why she wasn't on the show and what she made it mean. The core filter then became a view of her life, creating an illusion. Her perception of her ability to sing was from inside that illusion. The decision had absolutely nothing to do with her ability to sing, therefore it was an illusion, and her life was viewed through that core filter. Her dream to sing with her family was dead. She lived in an illusion, not in fact, and all of her actions in this area of her life were made from unconscious choice - by default.

Let's commit some additional time to looking at this place of core filtering.

Core Filtering creates the means by which we see life, establishes how we make choices, and is the basis on which circumstances present themselves. The process of core filtering is robotic in nature. We operate our lives automatically driven by the filtering process. We are unconscious to the process and unfortunately unaware of its effects. Though we may know that we must have something to do with the way life presents itself, we really haven't been aware of the role that we actually play in the creation of our lives.

We have spent years trying to convert our negative thoughts to positive thoughts in order to sustain a more positive attitude. Though there is definitely something to be said about positive thinking over negative thinking, generally we will revert to our usual way of thinking after a period of time. We are thrown automatically to this path of thinking. Not automatic by nature - but automatic by core filtering. Being negative is not the natural state of being. When we actually have the choice of living our life from conscious choice, free of core filtering, then positive attitude and positive affirmation are a by-product rather than the method.

So why are we thrown into varying degrees of this negative-thinking way of being? Core filtering is the culprit. Core filtering is made up of two categories of core filters. Envision that these two filters create totally different perspectives of life – illusions of different empowerments.

One core filter is empowering, in which our perspective and experience of life is one of pleasure, it is engaging, it is a life of effortlessness. From this empowering perspective we possess a yes-I-can attitude, we take action, and through this filter we experience the greater side of life.

Another core filter is disempowering, in which our perspective and experience of life is one of displeasure, resistance, and avoidance. We experience life as difficult, and filled with hurt and pain. Life just doesn't seem to work when this filter is running the show. At all times one or the other is running. We are always looking at life through one or the other filter: Empowering Core Filters (ECF) or Disempowering Core Filters (DCF).

DCFs

Disempowering core filters breed and perpetuate limiting thinking. We saw this a little earlier with Linda's story, resulting in limited living. These filters manifest our reality in which we experience the circumstances around us. These experiences are sustained by those words of doubt and by the mind striving to maintain survival from the pain associated with DCFs. All of our visions, dreams, and desires are held captive by the filters and their limiting thinking. Linda could not bear the pain so she withheld herself and avoided anything and everything having to do with singing. I would certainly call that limited living - living without the possibility of achieving her dream.

ECFs

Empowering core filters breed and perpetuate limitless thinking. These filters also manifest the reality in which we experience the circumstances around us. These experiences are sustained by words of encouragement, and the mind is totally absent to the need to be on guard. Survival watch is not needed. That is why there is such an awesome sense of effortlessness and life itself affirms limitless living. When ECFs are running, all of our dreams are possible and life works.

Let's look a little closer at this thing called core filtering and the two realms of choice. If we have established that there is nothing real and everything truly does come as a result of our perspective, maybe everything truly is in the "eye of the beholder." We can see life only through our perspective, but what is it that forms our perspective? It has to be the way we believe things are that has us create our perspective and our reality. This is where core filtering takes place. We actually view life through these filters.

In order to expand our reality, we must first discover our current filters so we can recognize them as the source of our current reality. They are the source of our reality because these filters - both ECFs and DCFs - influence every choice that we make, regardless of the circumstances. It generally appears that the circumstances in our lives are the direct cause for and the reasons we make specific choices. It appears that we really don't have any choice at all. It appears our choices are all a response to the circumstances which are directly caused by the outside world.

When we live life as if we are at the mercy of the world's conditions and circumstances, we are rendered powerless. However, once we see and decide that we do in fact have core filters and these filters frame the way we see life, define our perspective, and create our reality, we are then rendered powerful. Powerful in that we are no longer at the mercy of outside influences, conditions, and circumstances. Instead, we can clearly see them as they are - simply circumstances. We no longer have a need to assign them to ourselves personally. We can now see all the options available to us. This is what I call living through conscious choice, rather than living through unconscious choice.

When core filters are undiscovered, unknown to us, not in our realm of what we know that we know, then the filters are calling the shots through unconscious choice. Our choices are driven by the need of avoidance. It is natural for us to avoid DCFs, because the brain is our survival mechanism. Its job is to make sure that we don't have to experience painful situations again, the way Linda felt when she decided that she was "not good enough." This need for survival is an illusion – an illusion because we are forever on guard to make sure that we don't come close to these filters, while at the very same time resisting them as being the truth about us.

Let me give you an example. Let's say you have a core filter called "weak." All through life you have compiled more and more evidence proving you are weak. Possibly, you weren't picked for a sports event, maybe you came in second in most everything you attempted, or let's say you were always run over by bullies. Perhaps in your relationships you are sure you are not the strong one, or possibly you were passed over for that last promotion at work. Regardless of the reasons for not being picked or coming in second, all you can hear very quietly, somewhere deep down where you can not quite grasp the source, is a voice saying, "I'm such a weak person. If I were stronger, I'd..." All along there are people telling you what a good job you do, what a great athlete you are, what a great husband or wife you truly are, that you will make a good manager some day, but right now there is still experience to be gained. You can't even hear any of the acknowledgements because of that little voice, who, by the way, I call "our little critic," that keeps reminding you that you are "weak." In fact, it has such a loud echo that you begin to make choices called, "I'll never try again." "I'll just keep myself out of all situations in which I will not be chosen or picked or require me to be strong." Now the limitations and the realities of your life will begin to shift to keep you safe from the feelings associated with any condition resulting in you not being strong. Choices are being made through the avoidance of the initial experience around "weak." None of the circumstances since the onset of the core filter really cause you hurt and pain. It is the original hurt and pain surrounding the core filter that you are on a mission to avoid.

Here's another story that will demonstrate the onset of a core filter, the work of the subject's little critic, and the limiting thinking and limited living that have resulted from his view through his illusion.

Tom came to the workshop to discover why he could not make relationships work in his life. He was 38 years old and was getting concerned that he might be living the rest of his life alone.

He had always had a dream of a family. He was a good enough looking guy. Women liked him, but for some reason long-term relationships seemed to allude him. As we progressed through the workshop, Tom began to nod his head. He began to see that something was stirring inside. He asked me if he could share about something that he was noticing. Here's Tom's story.

When Tom was a really young guy, around four years old, he experienced a very scary and painful situation. He and mom were in the kitchen one morning having breakfast and his mom got really sick. She fell to the floor in front of Tom. Tom can hardly stand the memory of her lying there. He was pulling and crying and asking his mom to get up, but she would not move. His mom laid there for a very long time before someone came to the house and Tom ran to the door. Tom's mom had a serious condition that had actually taken her life. It took her life immediately, however, all Tom could feel was that he was "too weak" to get help, to help his mom, to make a phone call. He was "weak."

The reality is that a four year old would not be expected to know what to do, to know how to get help, to be strong enough to help Mom up makes no difference in the reality of the child. All the child can see is his insufficient ability to help. Through his perception, he made the circumstance mean that he was "weak."

From that moment on he was in such pain, which caused him to avoid all conditions that would possibly remind him of being weak, or cause him to look "weak." Unable to live with the pain over this core filter from that point on he did everything possible to prove how "strong" he was. It was a double-edged sword. He set out to prove the opposite, avoiding any condition that might result in the core filter of "weak" being exposed. He was in total resistance to the mere thought that his being "weak" was accurate.

He shared that as a young boy and teenager, he was always getting into trouble. He was the "bully" in school, trying to be tough and strong. In later years, he became domineering in his relationships to prove his strength. Eventually, he lost every relationship he ever had. He longed for a loving and nurturing relationship, but was totally unaware of why he could not keep one together. Tom was blind to the core filter "weak." His relationships were doomed before they ever got started.

Can you see that in every situation he was on a treadmill of failure until he had an opportunity to see the core filter? When he took on "weak," then he truly created a distinction of measurement for himself: Weak-Strong. All choice and all action for him had been measured unconsciously by the Weak-Strong distinction. Once Tom had an opportunity to see the filter, the unconscious choices he made to avoid the experience of this filter being true, he was then free to choose.

When he identified his filter, he could see the power that he had given it. He could see how he made unconscious choices through it. He saw his unconscious choice to be a bully to avoid the hurt and pain of being perceived as weak.

Today Tom is very conscious of when "weak" has him by the throat. He can see when he wants to run. He is aware of his sometimes overbearing attitude, which only rears its head when he perceives that he might be seen as weak.

You see, it isn't about him getting rid of that part of him called "weak." "Weak" is a part of Tom because he made it a part of him. It is truly about embracing all that he says he is. Because he identified something that he didn't know that he didn't know, and moved into the realm of what he knows that he knows, he has new power. He is now able to choose with new awareness, by conscious choice, and lives his life by his design.

When he lives and makes choices based on his core filters, he does not see all his options. He is stuck with only those options dictated by the core filters – usually anything that emulates escape, which is only another illusion. In situations where previously he was threatened by the possibility of being weak, he can now make choices that are not influenced by the illusion of weak-strong. He can see all his options rather than being at the effect of the core filter "weak."

An important note to remember here about perception: People do not perceive us as we perceive ourselves. In other words, these core filters are not seen by others. The need to avoid appears only to us. It takes place very silently inside. The very thing that we are avoiding is the perception from others and even this is done on an unconscious level. All of the avoidance is coming to us unconsciously. We don't recognize that the actions we take to avoid have anything at all to do with the need to avoid. It appears (the illusion once again) that we just aren't interested, don't like things, don't have time, all the "reasons" we use to keep us comfortable. Additionally, all the judgments and assessments of others are a derivative of their perceptions which is based totally on their own core filtering.

There is another old saying: "Don't flatter yourself. That person can't be thinking about you, how you look, or how you are. They are far too busy thinking of themselves and how they look." So true. The core filtering process has us all on a hook, and we're all sinking fast.

Oh, by the way, back to Tom for a moment. He has a lovely wife and awesome children today. He is now realizing his dream for a family. What caused the shift? Once he saw the core filter, then he could make choices in the way he related to others in all aspects of his life - relationship, marriage, and family, too, from a new place. He related from pure love and not "weak." Needing to be strong didn't dictate his choices. His limiting thinking shifted and he began living his dream by creating new circumstances in his life. He was no longer looking at the circumstances around him and falling victim to them, but rather taking great leaps forward and speaking what he was going to have in his life – and he got 'em.

So, if core filtering is setting the basis of our experience of life, and we aren't aware of the existence of core filtering, then what's the possibility of ever living a life filled with peace, less effort, greater experience of love, happier relationships, fewer upsets, a pure love for life, happier days at work, careers that make our heart sing, and finally realizing our dreams? (To just slightly scratch the surface.) I suspect that if we could clearly see that living our dreams is possible, we would certainly enjoy a greater slice of life. The greater piece of life isn't living a life that is different, better, or more, but rather a life where we can come full circle, embrace our core filters, and return to the pure love – the essence that exists only in the heart. So in the journey for a greater piece of life we need not be concerned about having to get better, but rather committed to getting back to who we already are, contrary only to these filters. The key to the game is realizing who we really are despite DCFs or ECFs - both are stories we have made up, and neither are real - while at the same time, being willing to experience both.

Living by Default

Take a deep breath. We are working on some good stuff here. You may be saying to yourself right now, "Well that's great for those guys in the examples, but I am fortunate and have never had anything so traumatic in my life experiences. I could certainly see how their situations could have caused them to come to those conclusions."

If this is so for you right now, it is very natural, and you are where a lot of people are in this part of the process.

However, if you are seeing it differently and you are experiencing that possibly you can relate, even though your life experiences are different than the examples, well guess what? It is very natural, and you are where a lot of people are in this part of the process as well.

Wherever you are and whatever you are

thinking or feeling is perfect for where we are at this time.

Just remember one thing, you are a participant in the outcome and not here to see what the book does for you or gives to you. You are the creator of your experience here, so play full out as we go along. As we create the picture and you share in the experiences of the other participants' shared stories, look inward to see what you are feeling and experiencing - NOT WHAT YOU ARE THINKING. The job of that thinker in you is to keep you from feeling, and it was the original feelings that you experienced that had you take on core filters in the first place.

At the end of a recent workshop, one of the participants came up to me and said, "I have never felt so much in my life. I could honestly feel everything that everyone shared. One of the most important things for me to take away from this workshop is the unbelievable awareness that I had stopped feeling." Life isn't really an experience if we can't feel, it is just an existence.

Can you relate to that? Most of us can. We stopped feeling a long time ago. I tell people, "To the degree that we can feel at all, is the degree to which we truly have the joy of living." Strive to connect with feeling again.

Let's recap what we've covered and move on.

- We can create everything right now and we don't have to wait until the end to see what we want or if we got what we came for.
- Dreams are an important part of living. Dreams are something greater than goals. We often set dreams aside in trade off for what is practical in life, or possibly even sell out on them, because we decided somewhere along the way that we couldn't have them.
- We have seen the possibility that we can reconnect with our dreams and actually live a life designed the way we want it to be.

- There is more to this thing of knowing than we might have ever realized. In that place of what we don't know that we don't know, may live some very important stuff. That's a technical term.
- We have learned to see that stuff is coloring our vision, that our life is seen through much more illusion than fact, and that we can give this stuff a name - core filters. Some of these filters help us to excel in life and some might rob us from the pure joy of the experience of life.
- We have also taken a look at the realm of conscious and unconscious choice based on these filters.

Here is something to consider: What if our intellect - our brain - actually leads us down the wrong path more than the right path? I thought I'd get your attention here. The brain, or intellect, is certainly necessary in maintaining and sustaining our very existence. I personally would not want to run along without one. But look at this: the brain can give us an account of everything that it sees, or perceives that it sees, from this very second backwards. It has no ability to tell us what is coming in the very next second, and yet, we often look to past events to predict future outcomes. By doing so, we then give it that power, and it creates our future.

What is in the past has absolutely nothing to do with what is to come except the thought and energy you give it. If that weren't so, then how could anyone have made it against all odds? The odds are nothing more than someone's predictions based on the past. Those odds are disproved day after day, and the only reason they are disproved is that those who beat the odds are the ones that didn't buy the notion. The core filter through which they view life, or at least a specific part of life, isn't a DCF, therefore the odds mean nothing to them. They aren't stopped by the odds.

In fact, the ECF that they view life through may be just enough to prove they can't be stopped. And boom, they beat the odds.

It is now time to get out of our heads, get into our hearts and start living from there. Our heads want to tell us to keep our fingers off of the fire. It burns. This is good and important, if there really is a fire. Unfortunately, it is also telling us to stay away from anything that might even come remotely close to any of the hurt and pain that was experienced when we took on one of these core filters. This is because the brain/intellect believes that the notions we bought into are the truth. They are not the truth, but only true to us because we say so.

Let's go back to Tom. Did anyone tell him that he was "weak," because at four years old, he could not help his mom and save her life? No. Tom made up that story. If we had an opportunity to speak to anyone in Tom's family, would they say, "You know what? It is true. If Tom had been strong he would have been able to save his mother's life." Absolutely not. They could have beaten their brains out trying to make Tom realize he had nothing to do with the outcome. Tom would never have been able to hear that. He was stuck with his own perception in the matter - he was weak.

When Tom could see the decision that he had made about weak, he no longer needed his head to protect him from that old pain, and his survival instinct was no longer telling to him to stay away from possible weak-strong circumstances. Whenever he gets close to those types of perceived situations, he can now see them for what they are and choose a different reaction - conscious choice. The bully doesn't need to take charge. His entire life in respect to all forms of relationships was shifted, and he began living his life from his heart and not his head - from design, not default.

Let's just imagine that your dreams are elusive to you because of these core filters - the disempowering ones, that is. And let's agree that this is the very stuff between you and you realizing your dreams. How do we get there? How do we begin to uncover these DCFs?

Through the remainder of the book we will look at DCFs more closely than ECFs because they are the ones that separate us from everything that we truly desire in life, leaving us living inconsistently with the love that we were created to be.

If this is all true, then we certainly are living a life by default and not by any consciously chosen design. There was a time in life that our dreams were, in fact, the design we had in mind. And this, for the most part, ain't it.

Are we doomed, or is there a way to find these little suckers? (Another technical term.)

There are lots of ways to find these little suckers. Get out your pen. You are about to get the answers. I smile only because I know that you have been looking for the answers all along. I know that because I left you in the forward with the possibility of getting the answers. Let's move on now. My humor is getting the best of both of us.

The best place to begin to find these disempowering core filters is to start with an acute awareness of that little critic in your head. We will get to know him/her better as we go along. For now, be consciously aware of what this voice says to you. You'll get to know this little critic in a new light. It may very well be your best friend along this journey.

Let's now do an exercise. On the left side of a piece of paper write your name. On the far right side of the same page, write down one of your dreams. Choose a dream that you have had a long time and not yet realized. At the bottom of the page, between you and your dream, write the words PURE LOVE.

Come up from there, to the middle of the page and write the words CORE FILTERS (DCFs).

Just above that write HURT AND PAIN.

Above HURT AND PAIN, write the word RESISTANCE.

Now draw a line all the way across the page starting just above the word RESISTANCE.

Above that line and at the top of the page write the words TOOL BOX, leaving space between the words TOOL BOX and the line above RESISTANCE.

In this diagram, you have your name on the far left, your dream on the far right, pure love at the bottom, on top of your pure love is core filters, and above the core filters is your hurt and pain that came along with taking on the filters. Above the hurt and pain is a huge amount of resistance. The line just above RESISTANCE represents holding and keeping down - your method of resisting the hurt and pain - so you don't have to see the core filters.

What is this tool box? When we come around circumstances, situations, or events in our lives and we perceive them as getting anywhere close to one of our core filters we slap a tool in place to keep us from feeling that OLD HURT AND PAIN.

So, what's going on with all of this? Before you took on core filters you were experiencing life from your heart, from the person you truly are. That is pure love. We were all created to be pure love. Somewhere along the way, we simply lost the experience of the pure essence of who we are.

Life's circumstances presented themselves to you, and you made them mean something disempowering about you. It hurt, and you immediately shoved the pain away. Each time you perceive future circumstances are coming near your core filter, you must get away.

As we discovered earlier, this is the work of the survivor in you. The survivor perceives that it is more of the same and you must escape. It is just another illusion that the new circumstances are more of the same, more of the same old stuff you so successfully packed away a long time ago. (Don't forget that all of this stuff lives in that part of knowing that we don't know that we don't know).

By the way, all core filters are all in place before we are even seven years old. From that point forward, the perception for the rest of life is just evidence that these filters are accurate, while we fight hard to prove that they aren't.

You think that you are threatened by the circumstances and suddenly, you are faced with:

- Anger
- Fear
- Guilt
- Resentment
- Withholding from others/going away
- Avoidance
- Attachments – the unwillingness for someone or something to go away
- Judgment and Assessment
- Confusion

These are the tools in the tool box. Suddenly you are really angry. For example: You are sure that a person or situation is the cause of your anger.

(Anger, being mad, being upset, ticked off, are all derivatives of the tool "Anger.") You immediately assign your anger to having been caused by the situation. Never once do you see that at the moment the situation occurred, you made it mean something about you - the you that the core filter represents - and you got in touch with the old hurt and pain. Faster than a nanosecond, (one billionth of a second), you slapped on the tool "Anger."

Let's spend a moment here analyzing what happened. A circumstance occurs. A situation presents itself. If your core filter(s) are threatened - if there is any possibility that you are coming in contact with one of your core filters - you immediately apply a tool from the tool box in order to stop the experience of the old feelings. Resisting the old hurt and pain surrounding the core filter is the intent for the use of the tools. Depending on your primary tools of choice, you will suddenly be angry; be fearful; feel guilty; have resentment; withhold yourself and go away; avoid others, places, or events; be attached to something being a certain way; or be attached to someone being in your life; immediately subject yourself to judging of yourself or others; or be confused. Every one of these reactions are tools you may use to stop the old pain. They are used to point outward for the cause, rather than inward for what actually created the reaction.

We use lots and lots of tools. A tool is anything that is a reaction. When we are living our lives in reaction mode, our needed healing and the appropriate actions are not revealed to us. We are totally running our lives by default because of our core filters.

This is a pretty strong statement:

IT IS NEVER THE CIRCUMSTANCES AND SITUATIONS IN OUR LIVES THAT CAUSE US THE PAIN. IT IS ALWAYS WHAT WE HAVE MADE THEM MEAN ABOUT US THAT CAUSE THE HURT AND PAIN.

When we are free of our core filters, then we can see all of our options. We are not living our lives through the mercy of the choices made by the filters, and the tool box is not necessary.

It is possible to live your life free of all those tools. When we make the choice to do so - see that choosing is a also a choice - then we are moving toward being 100 percent responsible for our lives. Remember from the first chapter? Not 100 percent at fault, but 100 percent responsible through conscious choice.

Remember Linda's story in the beginning chapters of this book. Each time she was invited to one of her sister's performances, to holiday parties, the opera with her family, or anything that presented the possibility that she might be reminded that she was "not good enough" to sing, she would slap on the tools of avoidance, resentment, and withhold.

As long as she could avoid the situations, withhold herself, and resent it that she wasn't gifted like the rest of her family, she would not have to experience the pain of "not good enough." What she was not aware of is that her filter of "not good enough" was a painful part of her everyday existence. The inside of illusion has another twist: the pain is there until we reconcile with the filter. The words of your filters are not the truth, as we covered earlier, but they are very real in your personal reality because you are the author of the filters - you made them so in your life.

All experience in life occurs inside of us. It does not occur outside, and the conditions for our experience are generated from the inside out, not the outside in. The circumstances and conditions in life are never the cause of the way we experience life, yet we live life looking outside of ourselves for the cause. We are then always living a life of default, powerless to the circumstances around us.

To complete the previous exercise, in the section on top of the line of RESISTANCE write all of these tools in that open space.

For your next adventure of discovery, begin to inquire inward about the circumstances by which you use each tool. Notice that I said used by you, not happening to you.The best way to experience this exercise is to create a page for each tool, listing the name of each tool at the top. Then begin to list:

- The things that make you ANGRY. What types of things make you upset?
- List all your FEARS. What things make you fearful?
- What things do you feel GUILTY about?
- What RESENTMENTS do you harbor?
- When do you WITHHOLD yourself from others, shut down, get quiet, refuse to be with others, or shut others out?
- What things are you AVOIDING? What do you not want to face?
- What are the things in your life that you are ATTACHED TO HAVING? What are you hanging on to?

- List all your little JUDGMENTS and ASSESSMENTS of yourself and of others.
- Write down those times when you feel that you are CONFUSED or don't really understand.

The purpose of the exercise right now is to simply get it all down on paper. Don't try to make it mean anything. The more honest you are the more value you will experience.

We'll come back to this later in the book.

With each page, each exercise, and with your inner inquiry, you are beginning to shift from living by default to a life of design - your design. Keep up the good work.

Filter Stages – Re-Connection Stages

Remember now, we are not working toward becoming better, changed, or different, we are actually moving toward being more of who we really are and that is pure love. Hence, the re-connection.

As we discussed early on, we are born with an amazing sense of adventure. The world is a kaleidoscope of possibility, of color, of movement. The sound, the feel, the taste – it's all about discovery. The best way to start off this conversation on the stages is to begin with the Discovery Stage.

The Discovery Stage

The first place we started our experience of life was in the initial discovery stage. Here we found nothing but pure unconditional love for ourselves and others - the pureness of the discovery of life, color, movement, sound, feel, taste, smell, and on and on. Here we found out who we were, defining ourselves through the exploration of others.

All is good until the first time you look out at a circumstance occurring around you and decide something isn't so great about you. As you learned earlier, the chances are pretty good that the circumstance really isn't suggesting or even implying that there is something not so great about you. Nonetheless, you make decisions about yourself that you determine are not good and life begins to change. Now you have entered a new stage.

The Danger Stage

Once you decide that there is a condition on your love or on you being loved, you are in the

Danger Stage. You begin to view the world from a place of distinctions. Most, if not all, of your evaluations are based on distinctions relative to you. You are now looking at the world though core filters.

Tom reached the Danger Stage at age four and Linda at age five, relative to the core filters that were demonstrated through their stories. (You will begin to discover that each of us have many filters, so to say they began the Danger Stage with the filter discovered in the examples could be incorrect. As they continue with their commitment to discover more of what they don't know that they don't know, they will find other filters.)

The age or exactly when you begin entering the Danger Stage is not important. Instead, it is what happens in the stage that matters. Once we take on a core filter, which is the entire basis of the Danger Stage, we began creating distinctions for ourselves. We then see the world with a focus on weak-strong or good enough-not good enough.

By the way, I am only using these two core filters because of the examples of Tom and Linda. There are many words that become core filters for people.

Once we take on a core filter we are acutely aware of the opposing word. The world is then viewed through the tool of judgment. Tom could only see his circumstances through weak or strong, relative to himself, as well as relative to others. Linda could only see where she was not good enough, and where others were good enough. The first tool we begin to use in the Danger Stage is judgment. The other tools soon follow as we move into the next stage.

The Danger Stage then, is the time in life that you are actually taking on core filters and the use of tools become a part of life - the life of default.

The Proving and Resisting Stage

When DCFs are calling the shots, you have a tool-based life. You experience:

- Wishing things were different
- Limiting thinking and limited living
- Unconscious choice
- Living life from the outside in
- A life of default - where our situations and conditions appear to be caused by our circumstances.

While in this stage, you are now on a quest to avoid at all cost the original hurt and pain present at the time the core filters (DCFs) are put into place. Life now becomes about proving you are not the filters and resisting every moment that might get you close. When you take on a filter you don't ever want to experience it again.

All the while, through the resisting, we make unconscious choices which create circumstances in our lives that actually give us more evidence that we are the very stuff that we are avoiding.

The Proving and Resisting Stage is a time of trying to prove to yourself that the filters are not so, resisting and fearing that they are true, and seeing more and more evidence that they are true. The cycle is endless and generally we are not consciously aware that it is going on. Typically, we are aware only of our anger, upsets, fear, guilt, resentment, our judgments, and assessments, (just to name a few of the tools). We are convinced that these reactions are caused by the circumstances, situations, and conditions of our lives.

Stay with me here. There is a way out of the apparent doom and gloom. In fact, the DCFs are pretty much the silent unassuming part of all of us. The little nagging stuff that robs us of all we can have in life.

So what's next?

The Way It Is Stage

There comes a time where we get resigned to the "way it is." We are so embedded in the resisting and avoidance that we don't even know what we once wanted. We don't even hear our hearts sing. We give up on our dreams. We may even forget that we ever had dreams.

We can clearly see that "the way it is" had to do with all those circumstances in our lives and nothing is really going to change. We are on auto pilot, dancing with all the justifications about why we no longer play full out. We look at the "if onlys" of the past and begin the coasting. It begins to show up in our marriages, our relationships, our jobs and careers, and can even go so far as affecting our spirituality. We basically shut down relatedness. Life is about handling all the circumstances that we created through all the resisting - limited living

Now what?

Being in this place in life can be subtle, a sense of not being happy and not knowing why.

Sometimes we may even look outside of ourselves and see that others had opportunities that we didn't get. In our finer moments, we find ourselves feeling guilty that we feel that way. For some it will be a knowing that the way they have been viewing their life may not be the way it truly is.

For me personally it was when I could see that there was a common thread in the circumstances of my life - and that thread was me. I began to realize that I had the same types of circumstances reappearing over and over in my life. Regardless of what I did, they seemed to come full circle. I even bought into the story that life's circumstances will repeat themselves every seven years. Boy that was a tough one to continue living through.

Wow! Maybe everything is choice and I can begin to discover why I make the choices that I make. How about you?

OPPORTUNITY OF RE-CONNECTION

- Making a choice to discover.

Re-Discovery Stage

Guess what, you are in the Re-Discovery Stage. How do I know that? You are reading this book. You are taking action to discover newly. It really doesn't matter what reason you have for choosing to read this book. You are finding that there are core filters through which we see life. Right now you are discovering that we have been living a life of illusion. These DCFs are not the truth of who we are and who we were created to be. They actually separate us from our pure love. They destroy our experience of love.

There is an awareness of the price we have paid in life by having the core filters. You are discovering unconscious and conscious choice. And that new choice is available.

Now there is a new perspective on those automatic reactions that just happen to us because of the circumstances. We now call those tools. We have learned that we think that they protect us when in fact, they rob us blind. There is new possibility. None of this knowledge was available to us when we traveled through the Discovery Stage the first time.

Transformation Stage

There isn't anything magical about transformation other than the fact that the pure essence of who we are comes alive again. I would have to call that part pretty magical. When we take what we learn and experience and alter the way we live our lives, it is transformation, and that is a miracle.

Here's one of those questions from the preface: What if everyone in the world could live his dreams? Here's a new question. What if everyone in the world could find his core filters, and no longer live through the effect of the illusions created by the core filters? The world would certainly be transformed.

Through the discovery of core filters, transformation becomes a conscious choice. Transformation is not automatic. When we make these discoveries, we get to choose to embrace them or not. When we choose to embrace them as a part of us, (after all, we were the ones that made them real) we then become free of the resistance and love ourselves unconditionally. Unconditional love is transformational.

Let's take a moment for a brief recap. During our Re-Discovery and Transformation Stages, we:

1. Obtain insights—discovering core filters.
2. Move the insight about the core filter from what we don't know that we don't know—where unconscious choice lives.
3. Once the insight is in what we know that we know, we can make conscious choices.
4. Breakthrough in transformation takes place as we permanently alter the way we live our lives.

The most important thing to realize is that the insight is not the breakthrough and transformation. It's when we apply the new insights consciously making new choices, that it results in permanent changes and you're living in the joy of transformation.

Never forget, above everything else, we were granted choice. There is always choice. Do you choose to see that and do you choose to choose?

Being Stage

Getting here is the life God intended all along. It is when we are living a life of pure love - living life through our hearts and not our heads. This occurs when we can appreciate our little critic for the part that it should be playing and it is no longer calling the shots. In the Being Stage you experience:

- Conscious Choice

- Living a life in the present - free of yesterday and tomorrow
- Playing full out - actually in the game of life, playing not just talking about playing.
- Having the experience that life is being lived from the inside out - rather than from the outside in.
- Experiencing passion
- Living creatively - living by design not by default
- Re-membering ourselves with who we really are.
- Living through compassion, the spirit of love.

When we are free to see others through their core filters, and have compassion for their tools of anger, fear, guilt, and resentment, we live FREE.

How are you doing out there? Stop for a moment. You are still the participant here. What are you noticing? Get that paper out again and write down the things that you are seeing. Getting this information on paper is important for you to capture the insights as you go. It is the nature of the little critic to help us to forget what we see. In other words, in order to survive the original hurt and pain, the critic must be on guard 24/7/365.

However, something that you don't know right now is that we are actually on a journey to uncover these untruths about ourselves. We are destructively living unaware of them. The circumstances we live are inconsistent with what is available. Our higher self - the love that we are - has the opportunity to bring us through to the Being Stage. We still get to choose. Your choice to write down everything you are noticing is an important step in choosing to live free of the core filters.

The Story

– Finding My Author

I have never asked anyone to do anything that I have not done, to walk where I have been unwilling to walk, face what I have not been willing to face, and experience what I have not already experienced.

Late May, 1985, Houston, TX

As I share my personal story with you, let me first acknowledge that I can tell it only through my eyes, through my filters, and by what I made the circumstances, occurrences, situations, and conditions around me mean. I clarify, because in most families, if not all, each member will have a different individual recollection of the "way it was, and how it is." Each of us determines our core filters uniquely for ourselves.

As I saw it….

It was a really bad morning. Why was I feeling so ill? Why was it that my sister was coming here from Dallas, and why was it that my dad was here? (Mom's not here because she died 15 years prior). Why was I feeling so lifeless and so emotionally distraught?

I was certain that my world had come to an end, or at least I wished it had. What had I done? Soon it started to become clear. I took pills, but obviously not enough. I was a real mess I really didn't think I could deal with any of this.

A week before I had it all - the perfect job making great money, three awesome kids, one beautiful stepdaughter, a pretty home, a new car, real estate investments - and I had built it pretty much on my own. And oh yes, I almost forgot. Six months prior I had married The Prince and I was sure that I was the Princess.

What had happened? He just wanted out. He wanted to move, and was leaving immediately to sort through it all. Those were the words I could remember him saying just before he walked out the door. There had been nothing I could do over the last week to try to get him to come home. And there was no answer to my questions about why I was being left.

I had recently changed jobs and this aspect of my life was on very shaky ground as well. Things were looking pretty grim.

On top of all that, I had even botched this attempt. This wasn't going to be easy - see this was the end of my fifth marriage. That's right, I said fifth marriage: Four husbands, five marriages, (I had married one twice), three children - each with a different father. After only six months of marriage, he was leaving me.

And worst than that, I had tried to kill myself. The only thing that I had accomplished was a worried family, frightened children, and a world to face that I did not want to look at. I knew that all the people who knew me and loved me wondered what on earth was wrong with me that I couldn't keep a marriage together. They would often say, "Belanie, you can go to lunch. You do not need a marriage license first." Oh, but obviously, I did need a marriage license.

It took me about two months to even begin to scrape up my remains and take a good hard look at my life. I had tried it all; begging, pleading, promising; and nothing worked. He was gone forever, and I was left without the answers.

In those moments, days and weeks, I had no idea that I would come to appreciate this time as my most life-altering event. I truly began to learn the power of prayer and the power of unanswered prayer. My prayers were clearly begging God to bring my husband home. I would do anything to have him home again. I was left to my own demise, failure in eliminating myself, finding that there was no money, the bills were behind, the mortgage was in default…now what? I had lived my life blind to what was happening around me.

It wasn't long before I realized that I had come to rock bottom - at least rock bottom of my life's experiences. Now what? That seemed to be the question of the month. Now what?

My first steps were to see that there had been five failed marriages and regardless of the stories I could share with everyone about why I didn't stay in the first four, I had no answer for number five. And he was the first one to leave me. In the previous marriages, I had been the one to leave. Regardless of the explanations of how the other relationships were and how they came to an end, I started to notice that there was one common denominator in all those marriages. Yep, you probably saw it pretty quickly, but it took me 17 years to notice. I married my first husband when I was 18, and now, at the collapse of number five, I am at the ripe old age of 35. The common denominator in all the marriages was me.

There's something I want to add in here. I was a pretty bright young woman in most areas of my life. This failed relationship stuff really didn't fit the pattern of the other aspects of my life. I had my faith in God, I was very good mom, an executive in the mortgage industry, a great friend, sister, and daughter. The list was endless, and nowhere did it seem to match my train-wrecked life around romantic relationships and marriage.

At this point, I was certain I couldn't live this way any longer. I couldn't put others through this anymore, and somehow I knew there was a reason for me to push forward.

It was as if a bright light had been thrown upon me in the very dark hole in which I was living. I know for a fact that this light in my facc was truly in my heart, put there by God, and I was on my way to re-discovery. I didn't know what it meant. I didn't know how I was going to get there. I just knew that I was on the way to an entirely new life. My Re-Discovery had begun.

If I was the one constant participant in all these failed relationships, then maybe I had something to do with the marriages ending. I had very strong stories about how "they" were. I had really come to believe my stories, enrolled all my friends, and had lots of agreement on how justified I was not to have stayed in the marriages. (Yeah, this is a victim's way to begin to see things more clearly, but it was a beginning.)

I had lived my life with no idea that I had anything to do with the way my life was manifested. It had seemed to me that we all hung out here in life, and everything out there dictated the way it was going to be. I certainly was at the mercy of what life had thrown my way. I was a good victim, though. I didn't hold grudges, nor did I feel sorry for myself. Until The Prince left, of course.

I remember the morning that I stood before the mirror and said, "I promise that I will be evidence that relationships and marriage work, that family works, and I am certain that I have no evidence that I can make that happen."

My promise was to God for the sake of my

children, whose lives appeared to me to be shattered by all the evidence I had given them that relationships do not work, only later did I find my promise was for humanity.

Somehow I knew that there was a love that was greater than all the circumstances in life and that I was going to find it. I knew it was a love that had nothing to do with what was outside of me. I knew with no evidence, that God was going to use me and all the circumstances that I had created in my life as a way to contribute to others. From that moment forward, the journey has been one step at a time. I first began with my own journey of re-discovery. I had chosen to purchase a roundtrip ticket.

That day in the mirror was 21 years ago. In fact, as I sit and write this "story" portion of the book, I realize it is the exact 21st anniversary of the weekend that The Prince moved his things from our home - July 4, 1985.

The road from there to here has not always

been easy. The path however, has been illuminated. I walked it with the light on rather than off, with a real sense of clarity.

My second step in the Re-Discovery Stage was to realize that I was single handedly 100 percent responsible for everything showing up in my life the way it had. That was a tough one to swallow, and maybe even a tough one for you to swallow. After all, we all know it takes "two to tango," and relationships are 50-50. No one person is fully at fault for failed relationships. I had lots of proof and all the evidence in the world that "they" were the problem. Nice people, but they were the problem. I thought that the choices I had made through all these relationships were made because of the way "they" were. It appeared that the choices I made were the only choices I could make.

For the record, let me say that there was nothing wrong with any of my husbands. They loved me. They were loving fathers. Any woman in the world would have been in heaven having them, but not me. They had good jobs. They didn't beat me. There was absolutely no reason to throw in the towel. Through the years we certainly began to make choices that became destructive, but in the beginning of the end of each marriage, I found every little flaw and began picking at them until they became real problems for me to live with.

Now, let me say this. This is the "100 percent responsible Belanie" looking back from here to tell you the story. It certainly wasn't the way I saw it as I walked through the marriages. I was so good at my stories that I had lots of agreement on how I shouldn't continue with the marriages, with the exception of only The Prince and Princess marriage. Of course, in this case, he chose not to continue. He left me.

Let's get back to my story now.

Given that I had discovered that I was the common denominator in all of my failed marriages, I had to get to the bottom of what on earth had I ever done that these failures were my fault.

Breaking the pieces apart one at a time, I began the exercise of finding the core filters.

October 1985

Slowly, I overcame the attempt to eliminate myself, had gotten through The Prince's move, the loss of my job, finding a new job, and now I was facing all of the financial issues. Life was beginning to move on.

With the continued support and encouragement of my dearest friend, Joyce, I took it all on. It was now time to stand up for the promises I made and begin to uncover the honest root of the way I viewed relationships. I catapulted head-on into the very train that I was engineering. I attended my first workshop.

I was committed to a higher quality of life, and with the help of my friend and mentor, Bill Ferguson, I was well on my way. He was there to make certain I had every possible opportunity to find my core issues, as he called them. I remember him asking, "What was it about the last marriage that became so devastating?" This was only four months after The Prince had moved. I speak of him as "The Prince," not because that is the way he felt about himself, but rather because of my view from inside my illusions.

Now back to Bill's question. What were the circumstances that made this last divorce seem so different, so much more painful? Maybe it wasn't who I was married to after all. Maybe that was an illusion. When I began to look at the relationship from a place of what was real and what was not real, I could then see that the marriage was really bad. Living life from the extremes, we were either madly in love or fighting with a brutal lack of compassion. Regardless of the extremes, I ignored the fights because I so desperately needed the love, and had to avoid, even at the cost of my dignity, the pain of ever being left again. In the moments of love, I lived almost in a state of worship of him.

He said all the right things - the things that were proof that I was not the core filters. I didn't know this. (Some more of what I didn't know that I didn't know.) My survivor (remember the little critic who talks to us from the inside all of the time) told me, "He is special and I am really special to him." Our entire courtship, engagement, and marriage existed for a total of 17 months.

All of my self worth, my sense of being pretty and my completeness seemed to be the result of the man to which I was married and suddenly he was gone.

As Bill patiently waited for me to look and discover the answer, it eventually came: The difference in this divorce from the other four was that I WAS LEFT.

I then began to see that the last of my five failed marriages was different than the previous four, because I called it quits in the first four. In the last marriage, The Prince called it quits and I WAS LEFT.

Wow! That was a huge discovery. I then began to see that all the relationships I had with boyfriends prior to any marriages had ended very abruptly - no reason, no explanation, no answers as to why. There was a correlation in the feelings my body experienced when The Prince left and when all the young boyfriends broke up with me. I then noticed that the ending of the other four marriages did not bring forth the same physical feelings. The question became why not? It wasn't that I didn't love them; I did love them. It wasn't that they were less important; they were all important to me. What was the difference?

Here comes the second common thread. My early-years boyfriends had all left me; The Prince left me. When I looked at these events, I could see that there was something about this fact that caused a very specific pain - a very physical pain. When I looked deeper, I realized that there was the same feeling around my brothers. They all left me - one for the Air Force when I was three, the second for the Navy when I was about eight, and my youngest brother when I was about 12. He got married.

I could see the same pain around those events. My body actually felt the same pain with all of those circumstances. I began really looking at that body pain. Did it occur the same way any other times?

I could then recall that it had always been very difficult for me to stand at the newborn nursery window in hospitals. When the babies would cry and shake in their little hospital cribs, I felt an uncontrollable anxiousness, shortness of breath, a feeling of wanting to cry, a pain inside. I would be so upset that I would have to leave the window.

The disturbing feelings that I felt while visiting the hospital nurseries were the exact feelings and pain I felt around the dating breakups, my brothers leaving, and my last marriage ending. "What does all this mean?" I asked myself.

Let me interject something important here.

The pain that I speak about are the physical feelings in my body. Each and every one of us will recognize and experience very different sensations in our bodies. We just have to begin to truly identify what is feeling verses what is an explanation of feeling. Cold, hot, rapid heart beats, sweaty palms, sensations in the chest, tight jaw, and anxiousness in the body are feelings. Upset, angry, mad, sad, having a feeling like you want to run, or hit someone are all explanations of how you are feeling, not the act of feeling.

Remember, once you are upset, angry, mad, withhold, and so on, you are already engaging with the tools. Once again, these tools are used to make sure you don't feel that specific feeling that was present when you took on the core filters.

Let's get back to the story.

Then I saw it. I felt the original feelings, the original pain. It felt exactly like the other pains through all the years. There was a real sense of panic inside of me, a feeling that I was physically helpless. I began to see. I began to feel. And I began to experience.

January 23, 1950

I was born to parents who were looking forward to having a girl, and a girl I was. I weighed, however, only four pounds, which created something that had not been expected. In those days infants were incubated until they weighed over five pounds. As a result, I was put into an incubator. When it came time for Mom and Dad to go home, I was not able to leave with them. They had to leave me behind in the hospital. As the circumstances unfolded, I observed the process of their leaving. I made it mean, "I am left."

To the best of my discoveries, over the last 20 plus years, this was my first core filter. This core filter went into place early in my Discovery Stage, when I was just a few days old. Interestingly enough, this set of conditions was so strong for me, that other core filters were soon applied.

"I am left"

"I am weak"

"I am a disappointment"

Certainly, a brand new baby does not know these words. It is a sense around the original feeling and we attach the words later on. The patterns are now set in play.

I am going to use this part of my story to connect the dots:

CIRCUMSTANCE, CONDITION, SITUATION

- Fact 1 - Baby is born
- Fact 2 - Baby weighs 4 pounds
- Fact 3 - Baby is put into incubator
- Fact 4 - Mom and Dad have to leave the hospital

What I made the circumstance, condition, and situation mean about me:

- "I am left"
- "I am weak"

- "I am a disappointment"

There were never words said by anyone that would have that be true. It was totally what I made it all mean. My life from that point forward became a quest to never experience the pain around those core filters again.

By the way, these are not the only core filters I took on during my Danger Stage, they were just the ones, however, that were at the root of this part of my story. As a reminder, when one takes on a core filter, it has the distinction of both the core filter and the exact opposite. "I am left" takes its partner "I cannot be left." I was on constant guard to make sure I was never going to be left again. The Discovery and Danger Stages do not occur at separate times in life. They occur during the same time periods once a core filter has been established.

As it all began to reveal itself, I began to share it with Bill, and I share it now with you.

Here are the pieces I can recall, and a demonstration of the unconscious choices that were orchestrated by these core filters.

As I grew up and people around me began to leave, for instance, my brothers as mentioned earlier, I can remember the familiar feelings and the pain attached to the circumstance. I always felt that each of the circumstances happening in my life were the cause of my pain. Add to this the stories around my boyfriends. All these events became more and more evidence that "I am left." The boyfriends' departures were all so unexplained, abrupt, and final.

I had my first long-term relationship at age 16. We dated for three years and married right after high school. First unconscious choice around the core filter that I could recall: This was obviously Mister Right. After all, if I had someone that stayed around for three years (I hadn't been left), then he must be the one forever - perfect grounds for a successful marriage.

Then came the real turning point in my life, and believe me this wasn't a good turn.

Very early in the marriage there were problems. Looking back, these problems may have been resolvable, but the real issue wasn't in the marriage at all. It was what I didn't know that I didn't know about myself: I am someone who is left.

In this marriage and my three consecutive marriages, as soon as there were real upsets, I was gone - out of there, emotionally finished, slamming the door on these relationships and finally ending them with divorce. As long as I could emotionally leave - be the one getting the divorce - then I would not have to experience the original pain around being left. I could point to the circumstances, say they were the problem, and move on. Life and death emotions were at stake. I had to leave. I could not be left.

One marriage lasted three years, the next three years, followed by a remarriage which lasted only a little over a year. My next relationship was an eight-year journey with split ups all along the way. In all cases, I made my way out first.

"I" was a double-edged sword. One side had to be married not experience the pain, and the other side had to be the leaver so as not to experience the pain. Basically, I was a relationship train wreck. I suffered; my children suffered; and my husbands suffered.

I had absolutely no idea that I had anything to do with the way it always turned out. From my perspective, I just kept running into the wrong relationships. It always had to do with the effect of my circumstances - everything outside of me. "They" were not bad guys, just not suited for me. I was not emotionally disturbed. I wasn't sick. I just didn't know the story that I had made up about myself a very long time before. I had taken on core filters, lived my life in total consistency with those filters, and made core filter-based choices - unconscious choices.

It is now 1984.

I am past the crisis of three prior husbands, four failed marriages and now I have finally gotten on the right path. So I thought. My life had become perfect. I had all the worldly things anyone could possibly want and I was about to marry The Prince. There was something different in this relationship. I was sure of it. I knew I was going to make a difference with him. In fact the day I left my office to head for our wedding weekend, I looked in the mirror of the elevators and I said out loud, "This one is different." And yes, it was. In a very short nine months it was all over. "I was left," and I was devastated.

Boom...the beginning of the end of the way I lived.

You have heard that story. He left. I took an overdose and flunked that test as well. My relationship with God carried me through all these times. I never felt that God had forsaken me. I never felt like I was being punished, but somehow I knew all along that there was something of which I was not conscious. My prayers and my commitment to knowing why I made the choices I made were soon to be answered. I promised God, my children, and myself that I would find the answers, and that I would be evidence that people can have relationships that work - that love and relationships do work. When I say relationships that work, I mean relationships that are truly lived from the heart and that we can become free from our circumstances regardless of what they are. Yesterday would not necessarily dictate the way today or tomorrow will be.

This brings me to the end of the way I was living my life and the beginning of the loving and empowering life I have lived for the last 20 plus years. I had no idea where that path was to lead me, but I did know that I was done with it the way it was. I had seen the core filter and the price paid by living unconscious to the core filter.

One of my most precious moments was when I was able to share what I had discovered with my dad. Dad and I were extremely close. He had his own way of being close with all five of us kids - a redneck country boy he proudly called himself. Mom died in 1970 and Dad really took up the slack in my life. When he passed in 1993, it was so clear how much he played both roles in my life. Dad spent many nights with me during all the divorces, experiencing with me all the sadness, and not knowing why I made the choices I made. More than anything, he loved me unconditionally as I walked that walk.

It was a Saturday afternoon and Dad was visiting. I had finally pulled all the pieces of the picture together, seen the core filter, seen the cost, forgiven myself, and it was the perfect opportunity to share it with Dad. He was sitting at my kitchen table reading the newspaper and drinking a cup of coffee. Those days, he was pretty accustomed to my flashing in, wide-eyed, and ready to share something that I had discovered. So when I came flying in calling out to dad from the back of the house, he was not shocked to see my tears and excitement. I placed my hand on his arm. "Dad," I said, "Oh Dad, let me tell you what I discovered!" "Okay," he said.

"Dad, that day, the day in the hospital when I was put in the incubator..." He stopped me immediately. Tears came to his eyes and in almost a defensive way he said, "If you only knew what that was like for your mother and I."

Oh my goodness, I knew immediately that I was right on. He went on to say, "Your mother and I knew that you were afraid. We knew somehow you were aware of being left. We felt foolish. There was no way that you could know, we thought."

But I did know. WOW! We had lived for some 35 years with something that stemmed from that moment they left me, none of us possibly knowing what I made it mean about me and the circumstances that I would create in my life as a result. It was more than amazing to me that for all those years we had never known that we had all three suffered that day. Suddenly, I was at peace. We cried together. I knew in that very moment. I could see that we all take on these stories. They aren't real, but we make them real, and our life's circumstances become what they are out of the choices made because of them.

You see, there are millions of babies cared for in hospitals at birth. Millions "are left" until they are physically ready to go home. Most important to know is that our core filters will not be the same. All of you wonderful parents out there need not feel guilt. We never have any control over what core filters are taken on by anyone at anytime. We do what we do, we say what we say, and each and every one of us makes it all mean what we make it mean. Notice, I did not make it mean I was unlovable, not wanted, not important, not good enough, or any other word. I just made it mean what I made it mean. That is all there is to it. Everyone has core filters. Some are ECFs and some are DCFs. The outside world does not cause them to be.

I knew then the purpose for me. I know it is to open the hearts of others to see their stories - to see what they made circumstances mean, and to help them return to the perfect love that they are, free from their core filters. Somehow I knew that this was my way to give back to the world all that I had taken - a way to serve God and humanity. God did not cause me to go through what I went through, but I believe he has allowed me to use it all to serve Him and others.

Through my love for God, my commitment to find the root of my choices, and the promise to be "evidence that relationship does work and marriage from the heart does exist," God gave me one of the greatest gifts of all - a marriage filled with love and joy. I met my lifelong companion in that workshop in October 1985.

To the dismay of many, there is another man

in my life. Doug is a treasure. He walks with me and holds my hand. He supports every dream I have and he learns to dream his own dreams. He is the very rock of support with me on this earthly journey. Our 21 years together have been devoted to a life beyond the circumstances, beyond the core filters. Once the core filter of being left was experienced for the last time, discovered for what it was, and I became willing to be left, I could then be in relationship for the relationship, not for avoiding or proving. That stage had changed for me.

I have not changed. I am truly just more me. I am living my life without the tools of fear, anger, guilt, resentment, judgment, attachments, withhold, confusion, and avoidance. I am free "to be" in my relationship with my husband.

Each and every day brings more learning, more surrender, more letting go and the result is more loving life. My commitment is to finding every core filter that stands in my way of living life from pure love and being everything that I was created to be, taking all that I learn and dedicating my life to offering it to others, that they might live free of core filters. We can all live life from conscious choice.

Living the Design – Lives Transformed

What is your design? What are your dreams? Reconnect with what you want to accomplish out of being a participant in the book. As we discussed in the second chapter, living by design is living free of the core filters and the tools we use to escape. You can design it the way you want it once you are past limiting thinking-limited living caused by the core filters. When you are living by design, lives are transforming, yours and the ones around you because they get you – finally.

Finding the core filters in your life is not the end, but rather the beginning. Once you find them you must be willing for them to be the truth about you. You must be willing for them to be so. It is in this willingness that you will no longer use the tools and you can live free of the core filter.

Hopefully, we have established that none of the core filters are real, other than the reality that you gave them. This is truly the beginning of transforming your life. You can then design your life the way you want it. It does, however, require more than the intellectual knowledge that they exist. The intellectual knowledge is only more information. If you could have uncovered the source of your discomfort there in the intellect, you wouldn't be here reading. It must be through the heart that transformation begins. Going home to the heart and healing these untruths is the key. Are you still with me? Don't forget you are still the participant.

I have met many people who have chosen to take this journey home to the heart, and it is with a great sense of humility that I share these stories of lives transforming and their commitment to living a life from their heart.

I'll begin by going back to my own story.

When Doug and I met, I was discovering my own core filters. He was in discovery of his. You might think that since I had uncovered my first core filter I would be done with it and life would be great. Well, I soon discovered that although I knew the filter, I was not quite willing for it to be so about me. Exactly one year and two months into our dating relationship, and believe me we were inseparable, I embarked on the next step home to the heart.

Since Doug and I met, not a single day had gone by that we did not see each other. Doug had a daughter from a prior marriage. He also had a core filter called, "not a nice guy." He juggled everything in his life to make sure that, regardless of the circumstances, he was always "the nice guy." By the way, this is impossible. Somewhere along the line he was going to show up as "not a nice guy." Given that I have a core filter of "I am left," guess what? You got it.

It was Christmas Day. Doug's daughter and

her mom had gone to visit other family during the holiday. Doug was acting strange, behaving not at all how he had always been. We had all had a wonderful Christmas Day and Doug announced he was going home for awhile. It seemed sudden and strange, but I thought it was just me. Off he went. The evening came and went with no word from Doug. The next day came and went with no word from Doug. This was absolutely unexplainable to me. I didn't understand. We finally spoke the next day. He said he was really busy and that he had to complete a long overdue project finishing his daughter's playhouse. Now mind you, this playhouse was under construction when I met him over a year prior. It didn't add up for me. But I thought, "Okay, if he needs to work on the playhouse, then he should be working on the playhouse."

Doug's daughter and her mom were due back in town on New Year's Eve afternoon. The remainder of the week had come and gone. It was

New Year's Eve day, and I had not spoken with Doug again. We had previously made plans for that evening, and I had no idea what was going on. Though I had phoned, he had not returned my call. I decided I would go to his home. I found him hammering away in the back yard, finishing up the playhouse. In a way, I was relieved. Yet I knew there was more to the story. You know, it's that deep down gut feeling. Yeah, that one. I sat in the doorway of the playhouse asking Doug what was really going on as he began to explain.

"I have made a decision to go back to my ex-wife."

I AM LEFT AGAIN....I AM LEFT AGAIN... THAT IS ALL I CAN HEAR, FEEL, AND THINK.

He went on to explain that his daughter really wanted them back together. The good guy/bad guy thing had reared its head, and I was once again face to face with being left.

It was New Year's Eve and I was home in my bed crying my heart out, for hours and hours. I was feeling that old pain again. I let it up and I let it come. I experienced it all until there is none left to experience. I prayed and I cried. Then the question came. Am I willing to finally be left and never, ever, ever have a relationship?

After many more tears, experiencing the pain, letting it come and letting it go, I come to the answer. YES. I am willing for it to be so that who I am to the core is LEFT, and to never, ever, ever have a relationship. Even in the face of my promise. I am willing.

This was the missing piece. I now knew that we really don't get rid of the filters, because we are the ones who take them on, give them life, and give them truth. "Getting rid of it" is what we spend all our life trying to do. Instead we must own them, not as truth in the world, but because we gave them life and power. Transformation begins when we own our filters, because then and only then do we actually stop the resistance. Then and only then do we stop creating circumstances in our lives in order to uncover our filters and go home to our hearts.

After the yes, I could finally be at peace, and finally fall asleep. This was going to be a new year. It was about 4:00 in the morning when the phone rang. I had only been asleep for about two hours. The voice on the other end of the line was Doug. "Can I come over and talk?" he asked.

I said, yes.

He asked that I forgive him. He had seen what a huge mistake he had made. He said he had explained to his daughter and her mom that his heart was not there. He had been making decisions out of his need to be a good guy, from resisting what he would have to experience if he declined his daughter's request to move them all back together.

I could see that it was out of my being willing to never have a relationship and my willingness to "be left" forever, that the shift could take place in his heart.

I forgave him, realizing how much we were in this journey together. I was finally done with "being left." We were married two years later. That was 18 years ago. Loving relationship works, marriage works.

Living by Design…Not by Default… Lives Transforming.

Debbie and Mom

"I am done. I can not take anymore of my relationship with my mother - not the way it has been for the last 50 years. She is mean. She has never said she loves me. I can never do anything right. She is critical of me and judges every action I take."

Debbie is the oldest of three children. The other children live near Mom and they say she can be difficult at times, but she certainly isn't the way Debbie sees her.

It is important here to remember what I said earlier. A family can all grow up together in the same house, experience the same relationships, and yet they will all see the circumstances differently. They will come away with different core filters in the process.

Debbie had plenty of evidence that her mother is the worst mother on the planet when it comes to being hurtful in her speaking as well as her actions. She carried the prize of mean mother. Debbie had tried to overlook her mother's behavior. She had tried to be nice to her mom in spite of the behavior. She loved her mother, but could hardly tolerate being around her. Though she loved her, she was never present to the experience of that love. She was always present to the experience of the hurt and pain. She would often say, "Thank goodness she doesn't live in the same state."

I knew it was time to go to work. And so we

did. Over the course of several workshops Debbie became willing to see what was driving her judgment in the relationship with her mother.

Don't forget that it is never the circumstances that are the problem. Sometimes our survival around core filters is so strong that we take a bit of time to give ourselves permission to see them.

Finally it all came together for Debbie. She was willing to see her core filter and take full responsibility for the way her relationship with her mother had turned out. She found the core filter of "not good enough." No matter what she did, she always saw her life through the filter of "not good enough." She often thought things would have been better if she had only been the boy that her parents really wanted. This was the story Debbie made up. Sure, Mother and Dad had said they had wanted a boy first. Debbie made that mean "she wasn't good enough." Everything that was spoken or done from that time forward was framed with "I'm not good enough." And the battle was then underway between her and mother. Everything was critical. Everything was about how she could not measure up to Mother's expectations. She never received any acknowledgement from Mother. Debbie closed down the relationship with Mother. She then saw her mother only through the eyes of "not good enough." She saw it. She was willing for it to be so.

Debbie could finally have compassion for her mother that she could never have before. She realized that she did not know what her mother's core filters might be, but she could certainly see that possibly Mother also had core filters. She realized that her mother probably operated totally consistently with those filters. Debbie could not wait to clean up her relationship with mother.

The most incredible transformation occurred in their relationship. Debbie sat with her mother and shared the fact that she had closed down the relationship. Her mother was so loving and understanding and they both forgave each other for all the years of separation. Debbie did not go to her mother, to give her the opportunity to tell her how she had done it wrong. But as she shared that she had made circumstances mean "she was not good enough," then her mother was able to express her sorrow for not being wiser and more aware in life as well.

That was about eight years ago. Debbie receives loving cards from her mother for no reason at all. Her mother phones her frequently and tells her that she loves her. When they are together, there is a loving understanding of each other. They hug, smile, and laugh together - not at all like the relationship had been for the prior 50 years or so.

Debbie's mother is now in a retirement home. I guess she's in her late eighties now. Just a few weeks ago, Debbie shared with me that she had gone to help move her mother into a new home at the retirement center. She and Debbie were taking a walk. Debbie asked her mother if she was afraid, and mother responded, "No. You know I'll leave here some day and I know when I do your father will be there to bring me to the other side. I want you to know, Debbie, I will be there waiting for you on the day you come to the other side. I love you, Debbie."

They held each other and cried tears of love, compassion, and understanding. Debbie thanked me again for her relationship with her mother.

You see, it is never out there. It is what we make all the stuff out there mean about us that robs us of the pure love and joy of life. Thank you, God. We can have the opportunity to see the filters and become free of their grip.

All those difficult years mean nothing in the face of the opportunity to truly experience the love in the present. Debbie speaks of her mother as loving, giving, and understanding, and that is exactly who she is in Debbie's life.

Living by Design...Not by Default... Lives Transforming.

Robert and a Lost Dream

Robert hated each and every morning, and wished he had different circumstances in his life. He had a great family, wife, and three adorable little ones. It was his job that he dreaded on a daily basis. He summed it up one day in the workshop. There was too much work, no time for home, no real life, always worry, and little time for family.

I asked him to tell me about his dreams. He laughed slightly, rather a smirk. His dream had once been to have a business of his own, but he had put that one on the shelf a long time ago. After all, he knew so well that most private businesses fail. He had a family now. He had to be responsible with a responsible, secure kind of job. He further explained that he made that decision a long time ago, the very same day he packed away the dream of being a business owner.

I asked that he consider the possibility that he packed that dream away for other reasons. He said he really didn't think that was so, but he would be willing to explore that possibility.

Robert could clearly see why he disliked his job so much. He was a department head at a very large company. His job description said one thing, but most of his day was filled with stamping out fires - constantly cleaning up the screw-ups of others.

As we progressed through the workshop and began to take a good look at the tools, he could certainly relate to several. These were primarily resentment, anger, and fear. It seemed he resented the conditions around his job, and was angry because he had to be in the corporate world. Every time he even remotely looked at changing jobs, leaving, and doing his own thing, he was gripped with fear. He was certainly in The Way It Is Stage of his life. Resigned to The Way It Is, his dream of owning his own business was long forgotten.

I asked Robert if we could explore further and see if we could discover a core filter. He agreed.

We began with the feelings that surrounded the anger, resentment, and fear. As we worked, he began to connect the dots, and suddenly saw his core filter named "screw-up."

He was only four when he overheard his parents in a heated discussion. He didn't really recall the words spoken, but his mom was very angry with his dad. His dad had made some poor business decisions it seemed, and the family was put in a very risky position. He could remember the words, "You screwed up," that Mom yelled at Dad. They lost their home, their car, and had to move into a very small apartment until they could get on their feet. Robert made all the circumstances mean that you must always be responsible and there is no room for screw-ups. He was terrified of ever making a mistake. It seemed that making a mistake was death for him. Not too long after that, maybe a year or so, he remembered throwing a baseball through the window of a neighbor's apartment. Mom was furious with him, screaming you have "screwed up." He immediately felt the same pain that he experienced when dad screwed up, and that, he knew, was not a good thing to be.

Clearly he was not a screw-up, and Dad wasn't a screw-up. They had both made some choices that had consequences, but the circumstances did not mean that they were "screw-ups." Robert was now the proud owner of a core filter "screw-up." His decisions were made through a filter of never, ever being a screw-up. He began to roll them off.

"I picked very simple subjects in school, stayed safe to assure good grades. In college, I would have loved to have pursued a degree in the arts, where my heart really lives, but those lifestyles are not strong and stable ones for family life. So my degree was in business. I got the first job offered out of college and stayed there, even though I really wasn't happy. It was the responsible thing to do. I really had to make sure I didn't lose my job."

If he had not been responsible, it would open the door to the possibility that he would have had to experience "screw-up."

Before the workshop was over, Robert got in touch with the price of his own aliveness. That core filter of "screw-up" really had a grip in all areas of his life. When he could see the price he had paid, he was willing to get it handled.

Shortly after the workshop, Robert shared that he had taken a new perspective in the way he related to his career. It was no longer a noose around his neck, but a career. He had become a manager, rather than someone who only saw other's screw-ups. This was a huge shift for him. A huge shift, because when we harbor a core filter, everything is viewed through that filter. At work, Robert was always proving how good he was at his job, and always seeing the "screw-ups" of others.

He later went on to include his painting in his life, with the possibility of owning his own gallery in the future - a business of his own. Someday, I am sure that Robert's dream will be realized because his heart is really there. Meanwhile, he lives a life with more fulfillment in his career, empowering others and now living free of the tools he used to keep from experiencing "screw-up."

Living by Design...Not by Default... Lives Transforming.

Josh - Job on the Line

The department manager (we will call him Jim) responsible for attendees of his company's workshop called me two days before an upcoming event. He said, "I have one person that is registered to attend the event, and frankly I am not sure whether I should have him come or not."

I asked, "What is your concern?"

Jim went on, "Josh has been with us for many years - about 18, I believe. He is an area manager of about 12 people. He really knows his job well, but he is terrible with people. It is a constant problem. We put him on notice, and I am sure we are going to have to let him go."

I asked Jim if I could ask him a couple of questions. "Certainly," was his response.

"Do you think that after the 18 years of service, the cost of the workshop would be miniscule if he could turn around his performance?" I asked.

Jim said, "Well, absolutely."

Then I asked, "If Josh does not turn his performance around post the event, would the price be worth it to know that you gave this otherwise dedicated employee one more opportunity?"

Jim said, "Absolutely."

Josh came.

The core filter Josh discovered isn't as important as our knowing the result. I received a call from Jim about a week later. He wanted me to know that they didn't terminate Josh. I wasn't totally surprised. In fact, he was doing incredible with his subordinate staff. Jim went on to tell me that Josh greets everyone in his department with a smile and real compassion - like a real person. This was something they had never seen in Josh before. He became a problem solver with staff, not a problem originator.

Living by Design...Not by Default... Lives Transforming.

No Balance in Life

One participant came because she had all of her life tied up in her career. She was driven to be the best in her career. Driven was the key word here. Once we identified the core filter creating this drive, she began to create order in her life. She began to live her life incorporating the things she desired rather than being driven in her job.

Today, 13 years later, she continues to be engaged in the programs. She sees them as an opportunity to discover all core filters that have stood in the way of her having every dream that her heart can imagine. Having the home of her dreams is just one of the many things she's accomplished throughout the years. She has overcome huge obstacles in her relationship with her husband and created a very loving marriage. She often tells others that if she had not discovered the core filters, she and her husband would probably be another divorce statistic.

Another of her dreams was to take her career forward to incorporate international assignments. She is now a large contributor to the international development of business for her company.

She dreamed of speaking fluent Spanish. She did just that. As a result, she got the fun opportunity to serve as interpreter for her company in Mexico. By the way, they landed the account.

Her dream to run a marathon has been realized. As soon as she reaches one of her dreams, she finds another. It's not that she isn't satisfied, but she lives as an example that you can live a life by design. Oh yes, as I remember back in one of her very early workshops, she did have a childhood dream to become, Miss Universe. I believe she's made it happen for herself. The Universe truly belongs to her.

In many ways, our stories are all the same. We discover. We make circumstances mean things about us. We see life through these filters, and make unconscious choices as a result. We give up on our dreams or at least some of them, and we begin a life of resistance. This life of resistance is a life separate from our hearts. In the process of trying to resist and prove we are not our core filters, we rob ourselves of our aliveness - the presence of our experience of our pure love.

Begin Now – Begin Where You Are

Begin now - where you are. You are in no need of change, just re-discovery. Start with your heart and make the difference.

Imagine if all of us in the world could realize that we are living our lives through core filters, which sculpt the way we "dictate the circumstances" by which we live. We are then on a path for a world free of:

- Anger
- Fear
- Guilt
- Resentment
- Withhold
- Avoidance
- Attachments - unwilling for someone or something to go away

- Judgment and Assessment
- Confusion
- And all the circumstances created by the use of these tools.

Imagine replacing them with:

- Compassion for Self
- Compassion for Others
- Understanding Self
- Understanding Others
- Empowerment of Self
- Empowerment of Others
- Unconditional Love for Self
- Unconditional Love for Others - Just Pure Love!

Questions to be answered:

- *Two people made a million dollars in the stock market. The market crashes. One commits suicide. The other goes on to make another million. Why?*

The one that committed suicide was devastated by the loss. Probably not about the money, but the core filter that was reactivated. He had no way of knowing that the core filter made the choice to eliminate his life. His core filter may have been failure, not good enough, stupid... In the end, the word didn't really matter. He just didn't know what he didn't know.

- *Why are so many of our teens suffering from image disaster?*

From day one they are looking at circumstances surrounding the need for a perfect body, attractiveness, and the stress that originated somewhere early on. Their little critic decides that they don't measure up, they're not good enough, not pretty, fat - again the words don't matter in the end. What matters is that they discover that the words are not the truth. It must be a personal discovery. They can't be told. Being told is a discovery in the intellect, not the heart, which houses the pain once they take on their core filter.

- *Why on earth are divorce rates rising?*

There are millions of reasons - as many reasons as there are core filters. Two people love each other. Broken homes are full of people who love each other. They just can't reach the experience of the presence of the love, because the core filters are actually at war with each other. Heal the core filters, heal the love.

- *Why are relationships experienced as painful?*

  The best answer for this question is to reference the example of my very own story. It best represents the debris - left over remains of a person's life - a life filled with undiscovered core filters.

- *Why are people working more, working harder, and enjoying it less?*

  They are not following their hearts. They are chasing the opposite of their core filters. They are creating their lives full of tools, and leaving their dreams behind. The voice of their hearts can not sing.

The list is endless...

Do whatever you need to do to. Begin now… begin where you are. It is the place to start.

Thank you for being a participant in this book. I am honored that you spent this time looking into your heart.

- Live Your Dreams….
- Turn on Your Passion….

It's a Matter of Choice.

- Discover your conscious choice.
- Discover the true experience of choice: A life lived from the heart.

The beginning…

What's Next

Roundtrip Ticket is the beginning of a whole new way of living—Limitless Living. To take the insights you've gained from this book and transform your life, visit us at http://www.liveatchoice.com. We offer a variety of workshops and courses, as well as individual coaching. Belanie is also available for keynote and motivational speaking engagements.

If you enjoyed reading the stories in the book, we have made it possible for you to read even more life stories. They will be changed and added to frequently. As a gift for participating in Roundtrip Ticket: An exercise in going home to your heart, you may visit this exclusive section of our website as often as you choose to see what people are discovering and how they are available to make new choices in their lives.

Go to : www.liveatchoice.com

On the welcome page click on What's New

Select : Your Gift from Roundtrip Ticket

Passcode : Choice

Real People, Real Lives, Real Choices... Real Reviews

Here are reviews of the pre-published book from people like you, who have taken a step on their journey to attain their dreams.

"Roundtrip Ticket embodies not merely a concept, but a roadmap for returning to yourself as pure unconditional love with your innate and incredible capability within to choose your life exactly as you desire. I am a participant in this journey, and without reservation recommend LIVE AT CHOICE as an integral and critical component to optimal balanced health for each of us. Choose your Roundtrip Ticket and live your dreams!"
- Mary M. Alavi, M.D., Founder and Medical Director of Balanced Health & Wellness, Houston, TX

"Roundtrip Ticket provides valuable insight into the human mind and how it can work either for or against our benefit. As we rid ourselves of one filter after another, our life becomes freer and happier. Our relationships become naturally open and loving. We allow ourselves to be successful in our endeavors and to accomplish our goals. Our possibilities for the future literally become limitless." - *Nicki K., M.A. in Psychology, Lincoln, CA*

"I am a nineteen year old from Houston; recently I had the pleasure of being a participant in your wonderful book, Roundtrip Ticket. It was truly uplifting, hope filled, and light shedding.

In the beginning of the book, from the very start, I had my first epiphany. As I was given the chance, while reading, to meditate and honestly think about whether or not I had any real dreams of my own, I was struck at how plain and maybe even boring the dreams I came up with were. I want a car, a degree, a nice job that I don't mind to much, and an average paycheck. Yep, sounds good. But after I put the book down and kept on thinking about the idea that maybe I had a dream, a real dream-the kind of thing that people dedicate themselves to, live for and die for, move mountains, and cross oceans, and combat every danger and hellish force they encounter for, It struck me in a thunderbolt flash that I had a dream to! A real live dream!
I jumped out of bed, grabbed my notebook and started scrawling away putting every detail of my wonderful dream down to the paper. And even as I have kept thinking about it over the past few weeks its become more clear, more refined, more beautiful. Realizing that I had a dream, me little old me from Houston, made my heart sing.

Thank you for that. But, it was only the beginning of the book.

Further on (more dreams realized) I found out more about myself that I didn't know-things that I didn't even know that I needed to know! Maybe, I am completely responsible for everything that shows up in my life. Maybe I am responsible for my own emotions, even the ones that seem to creep up from behind and victimize hundreds like sadness, and confusion. Maybe I don't have to live as a slave to the circumstances in my life. Maybe I have the power to choose, and maybe whether I know it or not, I've had, and used the power all along.

I even began to discover some of the things that have in the past cause me to take certain actions over others, even when the outcome was not healthy. I have found out some of the things that cause those victimizing circumstances to show up. I have begun to feel again, and to want to feel more! I have a dream of being fully alive, in pure love and in pure light and in pure peace of mind.

I know that, moving forward with my own journey, with guidance from your wise and hard found words, I can realize, fulfill, and re-realize my wonderful dreams.
Thank you so much for showing me I've had the power all along." - *Eric M., Houston, TX*

"Roundtrip Ticket really hit home for me. Belanie Dishong has written a thoughtful and honest book on the journey of self-exploration and discovery of our lives and how our lives present themselves to us. I used to feel like I was just a victim of all the circumstances of my life, but now, I understand I have this incredible opportunity to be the one who chooses how I want my life to be. She teaches us about compassion and understanding for the human soul and brings wonderful healing to the challenges and realities of our lives. Thank you for making a difference in how I live my life and how I make my choices to have my life be all that I want it to be. Her insight really helps me understand compassion and love for others as we all live in our daily realities.This book is truly a fundamental healing guide for living our lives fully and with all the love we can." - *Lydia B., Pleasanton, CA*

"Roundtrip Ticket is a guide to the self-exploration of events that may have prevented you from living your true life. It is well written, insightful and effective." - *Dale S., Houston, TX*

"This book is a must read for anyone who chooses to live life more fully and richly. I love how Belanie is able to stay so connected with her reader throughout the book. I felt like she was standing right next to me and supporting me every step of the way. I would have to say that understanding/experiencing our personal truths is one of the most important things we can do in our lifetime. This book shows us how to do just that."
- *Monica W., Oakland, CA*

"Roundtrip Ticket is an inspiration for anyone who has a dream of what can be in their life and our world. I've read many wonderful books that speak to living my dreams, living in peace within myself and in relationship to others and all that is our universe. I am grateful for the knowledge I gained through the writings of authors such as Joseph Campbell, Carolyn Myss, Depak Chopra, Clarissa Pinkola Estes and so many other insightful authors.These readings inspire me and I always knew what they were saying is the truth, yet I struggled to apply this knowledge in living my everyday life.Although I understood all of this conceptually and intellectually and always knew it was the truth, I didn't know how to take these concepts and bring them home to me so that it could make a difference in my life. I would change circumstances trying for a different result yet the same patterns seemed to re-occur no matter the shift in circumstances. The Unpainted Picture and Live at Choice provided the 'how-to' to bring these concepts alive in all areas of my life, my relationship with myself, with the universe, with family, friends and at work." - *Kathy R., San Jose, CA*

For more reviews, please visit us on the web at www.liveatchoice.com. Don't miss the chance to add your own review.

A life lived from the Heart

THE BEGINNING

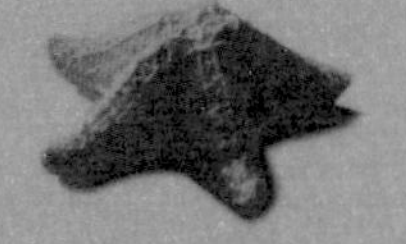

A life lived from the Heart

THE BEGINNING

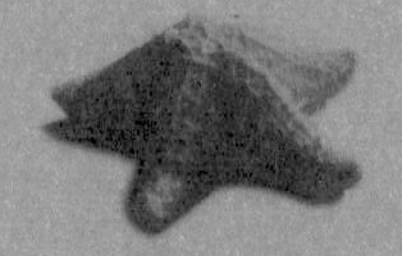